ANABASIS

Books by St.-John Perse

ÉLOGES

AMITIÉ DU PRINCE

ANABASE

EXIL

VENTS

AMERS

CHRONIQUE

OISEAUX

ANABASIS

A poem by St.-John Perse

translated and with a preface

by T. S. Eliot

A Harbinger Book   Harcourt Brace Jovanovich, Inc.   New York

CONTENTS

PREFACE

I AM BY no means convinced that a poem like *Anabase* requires a preface at all. It is better to read such a poem six times, and dispense with a preface. But when a poem is presented in the form of a translation, people who have never heard of it are naturally inclined to demand some testimonial. So I give mine hereunder.

Anabase is already well known, not only in France, but in other countries of Europe. One of the best Introductions to the poem is that of the late Hugo von Hofmannsthal, which forms the preface to the German translation.[1] There is another by Valéry Larbaud, which forms the preface to the Russian translation.[2] And there was an informative note by Lucien Fabre in the *Nouvelles Littéraires*.

For myself, once having had my attention drawn to the poem by a friend whose taste I trusted, there was no need for a preface. I did not need to be told, after one reading, that the word *anabasis* has no particular reference to Xenophon or the journey of the Ten Thousand, no particular reference to Asia *Minor*; and that no map of its migrations could be drawn up. Mr. Perse is

[1] See page 105.   [2] See page 101.

9

using the word *anabasis* in the same literal sense in which Xeno-phon himself used it. The poem is a series of images of migra-tion, of conquest of vast spaces in Asiatic wastes, of destruction and foundation of cities and civilizations of any races or epochs of the ancient East.

I may, I trust, borrow from Mr. Fabre two notions which may be of use to the English reader. The first is that any obscurity of the poem, on first readings, is due to the suppression of "links in the chain," of explanatory and connecting matter, and not to incoherence, or to the love of cryptogram. The justification of such abbreviation of method is that the sequence of images coincides and concentrates into one intense impression of barbaric civiliza-tion. The reader has to allow the images to fall into his memory successively without questioning the reasonableness of each at the moment; so that, at the end, a total effect is produced.

Such selection of a sequence of images and ideas has nothing chaotic about it. There is a logic of the imagination as well as a logic of concepts. People who do not appreciate poetry always find it difficult to distinguish between order and chaos in the arrangement of images; and even those who are capable of appreciating poetry cannot depend upon first impressions. I was not convinced of Mr. Perse's imaginative order until I had read the poem five or six times. And if, as I suggest, such an arrange-ment of imagery requires just as much "fundamental brain-work" as the arrangement of an argument, it is to be expected that the reader of a poem should take at least as much trouble as a barrister reading an important decision on a complicated case.

I refer to this poem as a poem. It would be convenient if poetry were always verse—either accented, alliterative, or quantitative; but that is not true. Poetry may occur, within a definite limit on one side, at any point along a line of which the formal limits are "verse" and "prose." Without offering any generalized theory about "poetry," "verse" and "prose," I may suggest that a writer, by using, as does Mr. Perse, certain exclusively poetic methods, is sometimes able to write poetry in what is called prose. Another writer can, by reversing the process, write great prose in verse. There are two very simple but insuperable difficulties in any definition of "prose" and "poetry." One is that we have three terms where we need four: we have "verse" and "poetry" on the one side, and only "prose" on the other. The other difficulty follows from the first: that the words imply a valuation in one context which they do not in another. "Poetry" introduces a distinction between good verse and bad verse; but we have no one word to separate bad prose from good prose. As a matter of fact, much bad prose is poetic prose; and only a very small part of bad verse is bad because it is prosaic.

But *Anabase* is poetry. Its sequences, its logic of imagery, are those of poetry and not of prose; and in consequence—at least the two matters are very closely allied—the *declamation*, the system of stresses and pauses, which is partially exhibited by the punctuation and spacing, is that of poetry and not of prose.

The second indication of Mr. Fabre is one which I may borrow for the English reader: a tentative synopsis of the movement of the poem. It is a scheme which may give the reader a little guidance on his first reading; when he no longer needs it he will forget it. The ten divisions of the poem are headed as follows:

I. Arrival of the Conqueror at the site of the city which he is about to build.
II. Tracing the plan of the city.
III. Consultation of augurs.
IV. Foundation of the city.
V. Restlessness towards further explorations and conquests.
VI. Schemes for foundation and conquest.
VII. Decision to fare forth.
VIII. March through the desert.
IX. Arrival at the threshold of a great new country.
X. Acclamation, festivities, repose. Yet the urge towards another departure, this time with the mariner.

And I believe that this is as much as I need to say about Perse's *Anabasis*. I believe that this is a piece of writing of the same importance as the later work of James Joyce, as valuable as *Anna Livia Plurabelle*. And this is a high estimate indeed.

I have two words to add, one about the author, the other about the translation. The author of this poem is, even in the most practical sense, an authority on the Far East; he has lived there, as well as in the tropics. As for the translation, it would not be even so satisfactory as it is, if the author had not collaborated with me to such an extent as to be half-translator. He has, I can testify, a sensitive and intimate knowledge of the English language, as well as a mastery of his own.

T. S. ELIOT

1930

NOTE TO REVISED EDITION

SINCE THE first publication, nineteen years ago, of the text of *Anabase* together with my translation, this and other poems of the author have extended his reputation far beyond the bounds of his own country. St.-John Perse is a name known to everyone, I think, who is seriously concerned with contemporary poetry in America. It has therefore seemed high time that the translation should be revised and corrected.

When this translation was made, St.-John Perse was little known outside of France. The translator, perhaps for the reason that he was introducing the poem to the English-speaking public, was then concerned, here and there, less with rendering the exact sense of a phrase, than with coining some phrase in English which might have equivalent value; he may even have taken liberties in the interest of originality, and sometimes interposed his own idiom between author and reader. But (to revert to the first person) I have always refused to publish the translation except in this way, *en regard* with the French text. Its purpose is only to assist the English-speaking reader who wishes to approach the French text. The method of the author, his syntax and his rhythm, are original; his vocabulary includes some unusual words; and the translation may still serve its purpose. But at this stage it was felt that a greater fidelity to the exact meaning, a more literal translation, was what was needed. I have corrected not only my own licences, but several positive errors and mistakes. In this revision I have depended heavily upon the recommendations of the author, whose increasing mastery of English has enabled him to detect faults previously unobserved, and upon the assistance of Mr. John Hayward, to whom also I wish to make acknowledgment.

T. S. ELIOT

1949

14

CHANSON

SONG

IL NAISSAIT un poulain sous les feuilles de bronze. Un homme mit des baies amères dans nos mains. Étranger. Qui passait. Et voici qu'il est bruit d'autres provinces à mon gré. . . "Je vous salue, ma fille, sous le plus grand des arbres de l'année."

*

Car le Soleil entre au Lion et l'Étranger a mis son doigt dans la bouche des morts. Étranger. Qui riait. Et nous parle d'une herbe. Ah! tant de souffles aux provinces! Qu'il est d'aisance dans nos voies! que la trompette m'est délice et la plume savante au scandale de l'aile! . . "Mon âme, grande fille, vous aviez vos façons qui ne sont pas les nôtres."

*

18

UNDER the bronze leaves a colt was foaled. Came such an one who laid bitter bay in our hands. Stranger. Who passed. Here comes news of other provinces to my liking.—"Hail, daughter! under the most considerable of the trees of the year."

*

For the Sun enters the sign of the Lion and the Stranger has laid his finger on the mouth of the Dead. Stranger. Who laughed. And tells us of an herb. O from the provinces blow many winds. What ease to our ways, and how the trumpet rejoices my heart and the feather adept of the scandal of the wing! "My Soul, great girl, you had your ways which are not ours."

*

Il naquit un poulain sous les feuilles de bronze. Un homme mit ces baies amères dans nos mains. Étranger. Qui passait. Et voici d'un grand bruit dans un arbre de bronze. Bitume et roses, don du chant! Tonnerre et flûtes dans les chambres! Ah! tant d'aisance dans nos voies, ha! tant d'histoires à l'année, et l'Étranger à ses façons par les chemins de toute la terre! . . "Je vous salue, ma fille, sous la plus belle robe de l'année."

Under the bronze leaves a colt had been foaled. Came such an one who laid this bitter bay in our hands. Stranger. Who passed. Out of the bronze tree comes a great bruit of voices. Roses and bitumen, gift of song, thunder and fluting in the rooms. O what ease in our ways, how many gestes to the year, and by the roads of all the earth the Stranger to his ways. . . "Hail, daughter! robed in the loveliest robe of the year."

ANABASE

A N A B A S I S

1

S*UR TROIS grandes saisons m'établissant avec honneur, j'augure bien du sol où j'ai fondé ma loi.*

Les armes au matin sont belles et la mer. A nos chevaux livrée la terre sans amandes

nous vaut ce ciel incorruptible. Et le soleil n'est point nommé, mais sa puissance est parmi nous

et la mer au matin comme une présomption de l'esprit.

Puissance, tu chantais sur nos routes nocturnes!

24

I

I HAVE built myself, with honour and dignity have I built myself on three great seasons, and it promises well, the soil whereon I have established my Law.

Beautiful are bright weapons in the morning and behind us the sea is fair. Given over to our horses this seedless earth

delivers to us this incorruptible sky. The Sun is unmentioned but his power is amongst us

and the sea at morning like a presumption of the mind.

Power, you sang as we march in darkness. . . At the pure

. . . Aux ides pures du matin que savons-nous du songe, notre aînesse?

Pour une année encore parmi vous! Maître du grain, maître du sel, et la chose publique sur de justes balances!

Je ne hélerai point les gens d'une autre rive. Je ne tracerai point de grands

quartiers de villes sur les pentes avec le sucre des coraux. Mais j'ai dessein de vivre parmi vous.

Au seuil des tentes toute gloire! ma force parmi vous! et l'idée pure comme un sel tient ses assises dans le jour.

*
* *

. . . Or je hantais la ville de vos songes et j'arrêtais sur les marchés déserts ce pur commerce de mon âme, parmi vous

invisible et fréquente ainsi qu'un feu d'épines en plein vent.

Puissance, tu chantais sur nos routes splendides! . . . "Au délice du sel sont toutes lances de l'esprit. . . J'aviverai du sel les bouches mortes du désir!

Qui n'a, louant la soif, bu l'eau des sables dans un casque,

je lui fais peu crédit au commerce de l'âme . . ." (Et le soleil n'est point nommé, mais sa puissance est parmi nous.)

Hommes, gens de poussière et de toutes façons, gens

ides of day what know we of our dream, older than ourselves?

Yet one more year among you! Master of the Grain, Master of the Salt, and the commonwealth on an even beam!

I shall not hail the people of another shore. I shall not trace the great

boroughs of towns on the slopes with powder of coral. But I have the idea of living among you.

Glory at the threshold of the tents, and my strength among you, and the idea pure as salt holds its assize in the light time.

*
* *

. . . So I haunted the City of your dreams, and I established in the desolate markets the pure commerce of my soul, among you

invisible and insistent as a fire of thorns in the gale.

Power, you sang on our roads of splendour. . . "In the delight of salt the mind shakes its tumult of spears. . . With salt shall I revive the dead mouths of desire!

Him who has not praised thirst and drunk the water of the sands from a sallet

I trust him little in the commerce of the soul . . ." (And the Sun is unmentioned but his power is amongst us.)

Men, creatures of dust and folk of divers devices, people

de négoce et de loisir, gens des confins et gens d'ailleurs, ô gens de peu de poids dans la mémoire de ces lieux; gens des vallées et des plateaux et des plus hautes pentes de ce monde à l'échéance de nos rives; flaireurs de signes, de semences, et confesseurs de souffles en Ouest; suiveurs de pistes, de saisons, leveurs de campements dans le petit vent de l'aube; ô chercheurs de points d'eau sur l'écorce du monde; ô chercheurs, ô trouveurs de raisons pour s'en aller ailleurs,

vous ne trafiquez pas d'un sel plus fort quand, au matin, dans un présage de royaumes et d'eaux mortes hautement suspendues sur les fumées du monde, les tambours de l'exil éveillent aux frontières

l'éternité qui bâille sur les sables.

*

* *

. . . En robe pure parmi vous. Pour une année encore parmi vous. "Ma gloire est sur les mers, ma force est parmi vous!

A nos destins promis ce souffle d'autres rives et, portant au delà les semences du temps, l'éclat d'un siècle sur sa pointe au fléau des balances . . ."

Mathématiques suspendues aux banquises du sel! Au point sensible de mon front où le poème s'établit, j'inscris ce chant de tout un peuple, le plus ivre,

à nos chantiers tirant d'immortelles carènes!

28

of business and of leisure, men from the marches and those from beyond, O men of little weight in the memory of these lands; people from the valleys and the uplands and the highest slopes of this world to the ultimate reach of our shores; Seers of signs and seeds, and confessors of the western winds, followers of trails and of seasons, breakers of camp in the little dawn wind, seekers of watercourses over the wrinkled rind of the world, O seekers, O finders of reasons to be up and be gone,

you traffic not in a salt more strong than this, when at morning with omen of kingdoms and omen of dead waters swung high over the smokes of the world, the drums of exile waken on the marches

Eternity yawning on the sands.

*

* *

. . . In a comely robe among you. For another year among you. "My glory is upon the seas, my strength is amongst you!

To our destiny promised this breath of other shores, and there beyond the seeds of time, the splendour of an age at its height on the beam of the scales . . ."

Calculations hung on the floes of salt! there at the sensitive point on my brow where the poem is formed, I inscribe this chant of all a people, the most rapt god-drunken,

drawing to our dockyards eternal keels!

II

AUX PAYS fréquentés sont les plus grands silences, aux pays fréquentés de criquets à midi.

Je marche, vous marchez dans un pays de hautes pentes à mélisses, où l'on met à sécher la lessive des Grands.

Nous enjambons la robe de la Reine, toute en dentelle avec deux bandes de couleur bise (ah! que l'acide corps de femme sait tacher une robe à l'endroit de l'aisselle!)

Nous enjambons la robe de Sa fille, toute en dentelle avec deux bandes de couleur vive (ah! que la langue du lézard sait cueillir les fourmis à l'endroit de l'aisselle!)

30

I I

IN BUSY lands are the greatest silences, in busy lands
with the locusts at noon.

I tread, you tread in a land of high slopes clothed in
balm, where the linen of the Great is exposed to dry.

We step over the gown of the Queen, all of lace with two
brown stripes (and how well the acid body of a woman can stain
a gown at the armpit).

We step over the gown of the Queen's daughter, all of
lace with two bright stripes (and how well the lizard's tongue
can catch ants at the armpit).

Et peut-être le jour ne s'écoule-t-il point qu'un même homme n'ait brûlé pour une femme et pour sa fille.

Rire savant des morts, qu'on nous pèle ces fruits!
. . . Eh quoi! n'est-il plus grâce au monde sous la rose sauvage?

Il vient, de ce côté du monde, un grand mal violet sur les eaux. Le vent se lève. Vent de mer. Et la lessive
part! comme un prêtre mis en pièces. . . .

And perhaps the day does not pass but the same man may burn with desire for a woman and for her daughter.

Knowing laugh of the dead, let this fruit be peeled for us. . . How, under the wild rose is there no more grace to the world?

Comes from this side of the world a great purple doom on the waters. Rises the wind, the sea-wind. And the linen exposed to dry

scatters! like a priest torn in pieces. . .

III

A LA MOISSON des orges l'homme sort. Je ne sais qui de fort a parlé sur mon toit. Et voici que ces Rois sont assis à ma porte. Et l'Ambassadeur mange à la table des Rois. (Qu'on les nourrisse de mon grain!) Le Vérificateur des poids et des mesures descend les fleuves emphatiques avec toute sorte de débris d'insectes

et de fétus de paille dans la barbe.

Va! nous nous étonnons de toi, Soleil! Tu nous as dit de tels mensonges!.. Fauteur de troubles, de dis-

III

MAN GOES out at barley harvest. I know not what strong voice has been heard on my roof. And here at my door are seated these Kings. And the Ambassador eats at the table of the Kings. (Let them be fed on my grain!) The Assayer of Weights and Measures comes down the imposing rivers, with every sort of remains of dead insects

and bits of straw in his beard.

Come, we are amazed at you, Sun! You have told us such lies! . . Instigator of strife and of discord! fed on insults and

cordes! nourri d'insultes et d'esclandres, ô Frondeur! fais
éclater l'amande de mon œil! Mon cœur a pépié de joie sous les
magnificences de la chaux, l'oiseau chante: "ô vieillesse!
. .", les fleuves sont sur leurs lits comme des cris de femmes
et ce monde est plus beau

      qu'une peau de bélier peinte en rouge!

    Ha! plus ample l'histoire de ces feuillages à nos
murs, et l'eau plus pure qu'en des songes, grâces, grâces lui
soient rendues de n'être pas un songe! Mon âme est pleine
de mensonge, comme la mer agile et forte sous la vocation
de l'éloquence! L'odeur puissante m'environne. Et le doute
s'élève sur la réalité des choses. Mais si un homme tient pour
agréable sa tristesse, qu'on le produise dans le jour! et mon
avis est qu'on le tue, sinon

      il y aura une sédition.

    Mieux dit: nous t'avisons, Rhéteur! de nos profits
incalculables. Les mers fautives aux détroits n'ont point
connu de juge plus étroit! Et l'homme enthousiasmé d'un
vin, portant son cœur farouche et bourdonnant comme un
gâteau de mouches noires, se prend à dire de ces choses:
". . . Roses, pourpre délice: la terre vaste à mon désir, et
qui en posera les limites ce soir? . . la violence au cœur
du sage, et qui en posera les limites ce soir? . ." Et un
tel, fils d'un tel, homme pauvre,

      vient au pouvoir des signes et des songes.

slanders, O Slinger! crack the nut of my eye! my heart twittered with joy under the splendour of the quicklime, the bird sings O Senectus! . . the streams are in their beds like the cries of women and this world has more beauty

than a ram's skin painted red!

Ha! ampler the story of the leaf shadows on our walls, and the water more pure than in any dream, thanks thanks be given it for being no dream! My soul is full of deceit like the agile strong sea under the vocation of eloquence! The strong smells encompass me. And doubt is cast on the reality of things. But if a man shall cherish his sorrow — let him be brought to light! and I say, let him be slain, otherwise

there will be an uprising.

Better said: we notify you, Rhetorician! of our profits beyond reckoning. The seas erring in their straits have not known a narrower judge! And man inspired by wine, who wears his heart savage and buzzing like a swarm of black flies, begins to say such words as these: ". . . Roses, purple delight; the earth stretched forth to my desire — and who shall set bounds thereunto, this evening? . . violence in the heart of the sage, and who shall set bounds thereunto, this evening? . ." and upon such an one, son of such an one, a poor man,

devolves the power of signs and visions.

*"Tracez les routes où s'en aillent les gens de toute
race, montrant cette couleur jaune du talon: les princes, les
ministres, les capitaines aux voix amygdaliennes; ceux qui
ont fait de grandes choses, et ceux qui voient en songe ceci
ou cela. . . Le prêtre a déposé ses lois contre le goût des
femmes pour les bêtes. Le grammairien choisit le lieu de ses
disputes en plein air. Le tailleur pend à un vieil arbre un
habit neuf d'un très beau velours. Et l'homme atteint de
gonorrhée lave son linge dans l'eau pure. On fait brûler la
selle du malingre et l'odeur en parvient au rameur sur son
banc,*
      elle lui est délectable."

    *A la moisson des orges l'homme sort. L'odeur puis-
sante m'environne, et l'eau plus pure qu'en Jabal fait ce
bruit d'un autre âge. . . Au plus long jour de l'année
chauve, louant la terre sous l'herbage, je ne sais qui de fort
a marché sur mes pas. Et des morts sous le sable et l'urine
et le sel de la terre, voici qu'il en est fait comme de la bale
dont le grain fut donné aux oiseaux. Et mon âme, mon âme
veille à grand bruit aux portes de la mort — Mais dis au
Prince qu'il se taise: à bout de lance parmi nous*
      ce crâne de cheval!

"Trace the roads whereon take their departure the folk of all races, showing the heel's yellow colour: the princes, the ministers, the captains with tonsillar voices; those who have done great things, and those who see this or that in a vision . . . The priest has laid down his laws against the depravities of women with beasts. The grammarian chooses a place in the open air for his arguments. On an old tree the tailor hangs a new garment of an admirable velvet. And the man tainted with gonorrhea washes his linen in clean water. The saddle of the weakling is burnt and the smell reaches the rower on his bench,

it is sweet in his nostrils."

Man goes out at barley harvest. The strong smells encompass me, and the water more pure than that of Jabal makes sound of another age. . . On the longest day of the bald year, praising the earth under grass, I know not what being of strength has followed my pace. And the Dead under the sand and the urine and the salt of the earth, it is done with these as with the husks whereof the grain was given to the fowls. And my soul, my soul keeps loud vigil at the portals of death — but say to the Prince to be still: on the point of a lance, amongst us,

this horse's skull!

I V

C'EST là le train du monde et je n'ai que du bien
à en dire — Fondation de la ville. Pierre et bronze. Des
feux de ronces à l'aurore
      mirent à nu ces grandes
      pierres vertes et huileuses comme des fonds de tem-
ples, de latrines,
      et le navigateur en mer atteint de nos fumées vit que
la terre, jusqu'au faîte, avait changé d'image (de grands
écobuages vus du large et ces travaux de captation d'eaux
vives en montagne).

I V

SUCH is the way of the world and I have nothing but good to say of it. — Foundation of the City. Stone and bronze. Thorn fires at dawn

bared these great

green stones, and viscid like the bases of temples, of latrines,

and the mariner at sea whom our smoke reached saw that the earth to the summit had changed its form (great tracts of burnt-over land seen afar and these operations of channelling the living waters on the mountains).

Ainsi la ville fut fondée et placée au matin sous les labiales d'un nom pur. Les campements s'annulent aux collines! Et nous qui sommes là sur les galeries de bois,

 tête nue et pieds nus dans la fraîcheur du monde,

 qu'avons-nous donc à rire, mais qu'avons-nous à rire, sur nos sièges, pour un débarquement de filles et de mules?

 et qu'est-ce à dire, depuis l'aube, de tout ce peuple sous les voiles? — Des arrivages de farines!.. Et les vaisseaux plus hauts qu'Ilion sous le paon blanc du ciel, ayant franchi la barre, s'arrêtaient

 en ce point mort où flotte un âne mort. (Il s'agit d'arbitrer ce fleuve pâle, sans destin, d'une couleur de sauterelles écrasées dans leur sève.)

 Au grand bruit frais de l'autre rive, les forgerons sont maîtres de leurs feux! Les claquements du fouet déchargent aux rues neuves des tombereaux de malheurs inéclos. O mules, nos ténèbres sous le sabre de cuivre! quatre têtes rétives au nœud du poing font un vivant corymbe sur l'azur. Les fondateurs d'asiles s'arrêtent sous un arbre et les idées leur viennent pour le choix des terrains. Ils m'enseignent le sens et la destination des bâtiments: face honorée, face muette; les galeries de latérite, les vestibules de pierre noire et les piscines d'ombre claire pour bibliothèques; des constructions très fraîches pour les produits pharmaceutiques. Et puis s'en viennent les banquiers qui sifflent dans leurs clefs. Et déjà par les rues un homme chantait seul, de

Thus was the City founded and placed in the morning under the labials of a holy name. The encampments are razed from the hills! And we who are there in the wooden galleries,

head bare and foot bare in the freshness of the world,

what have we to laugh at, but what have we to laugh at, as we sit, for a disembarkation of girls and mules?

and what is there to say, since the dawn, of all this people under sail? — Arrivals of grain! . . And the ships taller than Ilion under the white peacock of heaven, having crossed the bar, hove to

in this deadwater where floats a dead ass. (We must ordain the fate of this pale meaningless river, colour of grasshoppers crushed in their sap.)

In the great fresh noise of the yonder bank, the blacksmiths are masters of their fires! The cracking of whips in the new streets unloads whole wainsful of unhatched evils. O mules, our shadows under the copper sword! four restive heads knotted to the fist make a living cluster against the blue. The founders of asylums meet beneath a tree and find their ideas for the choice of situations. They teach me the meaning and the purpose of the buildings: front adorned, back blind; the galleries of laterite, the vestibules of black stone and the pools of clear shadow for libraries; cool places for wares of the druggist. And then come the bankers blowing into their keys. And already in the streets a man sang alone, one of those who paint on their brow the cipher of their god. (Perpetual crackling of insects in this quarter of

43

ceux qui peignent sur leur front le chiffre de leur Dieu. (*Crépitements d'insectes à jamais dans ce quartier aux détritus!*) . . Et ce n'est point le lieu de vous conter nos alliances avec les gens de l'autre rive; l'eau offerte dans des outres, les prestations de cavalerie pour les travaux du port et les princes payés en monnaie de poissons. (*Un enfant triste comme la mort des singes — sœur aînée d'une grande beauté — nous offrait une caille dans un soulier de satin rose.*)

   . . . Solitude! l'œuf bleu que pond un grand oiseau de mer, et les baies au matin tout encombrées de citrons d'or! — C'était hier! L'oiseau s'en fut!

   Demain les fêtes, les clameurs, les avenues plantées d'arbres à gousses et les services de voierie emportant à l'aurore de grands morceaux de palmes mortes, débris d'ailes géantes. . . Demain les fêtes,

   les élections de magistrats du port, les vocalises aux banlieues et, sous les tièdes couvaisons d'orage,

   la ville jaune, casquée d'ombre, avec ses caleçons de filles aux fenêtres.

*
* *

   . . . A la troisième lunaison, ceux qui veillaient aux crêtes des collines replièrent leurs toiles. On fit brûler un corps de femme dans les sables. Et un homme s'avança à l'entrée du Désert — profession de son père: marchand de flacons.

44

vacant lots and rubbish.) . . And this is no time to tell you, no time to reckon our alliances with the people of the other shore; water presented in skins, commandeering of cavalry for the dock-works and princes paid in currency of fish. (A child sorrowful as the death of apes — one that had an elder sister of great beauty — offered us a quail in a slipper of rose-coloured satin.)

. . . Solitude! the blue egg laid by a great sea-bird, and the bays at morning all littered with gold lemons! — Yesterday it was! The bird made off!

Tomorrow the festivals and tumults, the avenues planted with podded trees, and the dustmen at dawn bearing away huge pieces of dead palmtrees, fragments of giant wings. . . Tomorrow the festivals,

the election of harbour-masters, the voices practising in the suburbs and, under the moist incubation of storms,

the yellow town, casque'd in shade, with the girls' drawers hanging at the windows.

*
* *

. . . At the third lunation, those who kept watch on the hilltops folded their canvas. The body of a woman was burnt in the sands. And a man strode forth at the threshold of the desert — profession of his father: dealer in scent-bottles.

45

V

*P*OUR *mon âme mêlée aux affaires lointaines,
cent feux de villes avivés par l'aboiement des chiens. . .*

*Solitude! nos partisans extravagants nous vantaient
nos façons, mais nos pensées déjà campaient sous d'autres
murs:*

*"Je n'ai dit à personne d'attendre. . . Je vous
hais tous avec douceur. . . Et qu'est-ce à dire de ce chant
que vous tirez de nous? . ."*

*Duc d'un peuple d'images à conduire aux Mers
Mortes, où trouver l'eau nocturne qui lavera nos yeux?*

V

For my soul engaged in far matters, in towns an hundred fires revived by the barking of dogs. . .

Solitude! our immoderate partisans boasted of our ways, but our thoughts were already encamped beneath other walls:

"I have told no one to wait. . . I hate you all, gently. . . . And what is to be said of this song that you elicit from us? . ."

Leader of a people of dreams to be led to the Dead Seas, where shall I find the water of night that shall bathe our eyes?

Solitude!... Des compagnies d'étoiles passent au bord du monde, s'annexant aux cuisines un astre domestique.

Les Rois Confédérés du ciel mènent la guerre sur mon toit et, maîtres des hauteurs, y établissent leurs bivacs.

Que j'aille seul avec les souffles de la nuit, parmi les Princes pamphlétaires, parmi les chutes de Biélides!...

Ame jointe en silence au bitume des Mortes! cousues d'aiguilles nos paupières! louée l'attente sous nos cils!

La nuit donne son lait, qu'on y prenne bien garde! et qu'un doigt de miel longe les lèvres du prodigue:

"... Fruit de la femme, ô Sabéenne!..." Trahissant l'âme la moins sobre et soulevé des pures pestilences de la nuit,

je m'élèverai dans mes pensées contre l'activité du songe; je m'en irai avec les oies sauvages, dans l'odeur fade du matin!..

— Ha! quand l'étoile s'annuitait au quartier des servantes, savions-nous que déjà tant de lances nouvelles

poursuivaient au désert les silicates de l'Eté? "Aurore, vous contiez..." Ablutions aux rives des Mers Mortes!

Ceux qui ont couché nus dans l'immense saison se lèvent en foule sur la terre — se lèvent en foules et s'écrient

que ce monde est insane!.. Le vieillard bouge des paupières dans la lumière jaune; la femme s'étire sur son ongle;

Solitude! . . squadrons of stars pass the edge of the world, enlisting from the kitchens a homely star.

The Confederate Kings of Heaven make war over my roof and, lords of the high places, set there their bivouacs.

Let me go alone with the airs of the night, among the pamphleteering Princes, among the falling Bielides! . .

Soul united in silence to the bitumen of the Dead! our eyelids sewn with needles! praised be the waiting under our eyelids!

The night gives its milk, O take heed! let a honeyed finger touch the lips of the prodigal:

". . . Fruit of woman, O Sabaean! . ." Betraying the least sober soul and roused from the pure pestilences of night,

in my thoughts I will protest against the activity of dream; I shall be off with the wild geese, in the sick smell of morning! . .

Ah when the star was benighted in the servant-girls' quarters, did we know that already so many new spears

pursued in the desert the silicates of Summer? "Dawn, you were saying . . ." Ablutions on the banks of the Dead Seas!

Those who lay naked in the enormous season arise in crowd on the earth — arise in crowds and cry out

that this world is mad! . . The old man stirs his eyelids in the yellow light; the woman extends herself from nail to nail;

and the gummed colt thrusts his bearded chin into the

et le poulain poisseux met son menton barbu dans la main de l'enfant, qui ne rêve pas encore de lui crever un œil. . .

"Solitude! Je n'ai dit à personne d'attendre. . . Je m'en irai par là quand je voudrai . . ." — Et l'Étranger tout habillé

de ses pensées nouvelles, se fait encore des partisans dans les voies du silence: son œil est plein d'une salive,

il n'y a plus en lui substance d'homme. Et la terre en ses graines ailées, comme un poète en ses propos, voyage. . .

hand of the child, to whom it does not yet occur to knock out one of his eyes. . .

"Solitude! I have told no one to wait. . . I shall go away in that direction when I wish . . ." — And the Stranger clothed

in his new thoughts, acquires still more partisans in the ways of silence: his eye is full of a sort of spittle,

there is no more substance of man in him. And the earth in its winged seeds, like a poet in his thoughts, travels. . .

V I

*T*OUT-*PUISSANTS dans nos grands gouverne-
ments militaires, avec nos filles parfumées qui se vêtaient
d'un souffle, ces tissus,*

    nous établîmes en haut lieu nos pièges au bonheur.

    *Abondance et bien-être, bonheur! Aussi longtemps
nos verres où la glace pouvait chanter comme Memnon. . .*

    *Et fourvoyant à l'angle des terrasses une mêlée
d'éclairs, de grands plats d'or aux mains des filles de service
fauchaient l'ennui des sables aux limites du monde.*

    Puis ce fut une année de souffles en Ouest et, sur nos

VI

OMNIPOTENT in our great military governments,
with our scented girls clad in a breath of silk webs,

we set in high places our springes for happiness.

Plenty and well-being, happiness! For so long the ice
sang in our glasses, like Memnon. . .

And deflecting a crossing of lights to the corners of ter-
races, great chargers of gold held up by the handmaidens, smote
the weariness of the sands, at the confines of the world.

Then came a year of wind in the west and, on our roofs
weighted with black stones, all the business of bright cloths aban-

toits lestés de pierres noires, tout un propos de toiles vives
adonnées au délice du large. Les cavaliers au fil des caps,
assaillis d'aigles lumineuses et nourrissant à bout de lances
les catastrophes pures du beau temps, publiaient sur les
mers une ardente chronique:

Certes! une histoire pour les hommes, un chant de
force pour les hommes, comme un frémissement du large
dans un arbre de fer! . . lois données sur d'autres rives, et
les alliances par les femmes au sein des peuples dissolus; de
grands pays vendus à la criée sous l'inflation solaire, les
hauts plateaux pacifiés et les provinces mises à prix dans
l'odeur solennelle des roses. . .

Ceux-là qui en naissant n'ont point flairé de telle
braise, qu'ont-ils à faire parmi nous? et se peut-il qu'ils aient
commerce de vivants? "C'est votre affaire et non la mienne
de régner sur l'absence . . ." Pour nous qui étions là, nous
produisîmes aux frontières des accidents extraordinaires, et
nous portant dans nos actions à la limite de nos forces, notre
joie parmi vous fut une très grande joie:

.   "Je connais cette race établie sur les pentes: cava-
liers démontés dans les cultures vivrières. Allez et dites à
ceux-là: un immense péril à courir avec nous! des actions
sans nombre et sans mesure, des volontés puissantes et dis-
sipatrices et le pouvoir de l'homme consommé comme la
grappe dans la vigne. . . Allez et dites bien: nos habi-
tudes de violence, nos chevaux sobres et rapides sur les
semences de révoltes et nos casques flairés par la fureur du

doned to the delight of wide spaces. The horsemen on the crest of the capes, battered by luminous eagles, and feeding on their spear-tips the pure disasters of sunshine, published over the seas a fiery bulletin:

Surely a history for men, a song of strength for men, like a shudder of space shaking an iron tree! . . laws enacted upon other shores, alliances by marriage in the midst of dissolute peoples, great territories auctioned away beneath the inflation of the Sun, the highlands subdued and the provinces priced in the solemn odour of roses. . .

They who at birth have not sniffed such embers, what have they to do with us? Can they have commerce with the living? "It is your business, not mine, to rule over absence . . ." For us who were there, we caused at the frontiers exceptional accidents, and pushing ourselves in our actions to the end of our strength, our joy amongst you was a very great joy:

"I know this folk squatting on the slopes, horsemen dismounted among the food crops. Go say to them: a great risk to run with us! deeds innumerable unmeasured, puissant and destructive wills, and the power of man absorbed like the cluster in the vine. . . Go and say truly: our habits of violence, our horses abstemious and swift upon the seeds of sedition and our helmets sniffed by the fury of the day. . . In the exhausted countries where the ways of life are to be remade, so many families to be composed like cages of whistling birds, you shall see us, the way we do, gatherers of nations under vast shelters, readers

jour. . . Aux pays épuisés où les coutumes sont à repren-
dre, tant de familles à composer comme des encagées d'oi-
seaux siffleurs, vous nous verrez, dans nos façons d'agir, as-
sembleurs de nations sous de vastes hangars, lecteurs de
bulles à voix haute, et vingt peuples sous nos lois parlant
toutes les langues. . .

"Et déjà vous savez l'histoire de leur goût: les capi-
taines pauvres dans les voies immortelles, les notables en
foule venus pour nous saluer, toute la population virile de
l'année avec ses dieux sur des bâtons, et les princes déchus
dans les sables du Nord, leurs filles tributaires nous prodi-
guant les assurances de leur foi, et le Maître qui dit: j'ai foi
dans ma fortune. . .

"Ou bien vous leur contez les choses de la paix: aux
pays infestés de bien-être une odeur de forum et de femmes
nubiles, les monnaies jaunes, timbre pur, maniées sous les
palmes, et les peuples en marche sur de fortes épices — do-
tations militaires, grands trafics d'influence à la barbe des
fleuves, l'hommage d'un puissant voisin assis à l'ombre de
ses filles et les messages échangés sur des lamelles d'or, les
traités d'amitié et de délimitation, les conventions de peuple
à peuple pour des barrages de rivières, et les tributs levés
dans les pays enthousiasmés! (constructions de citernes, de
granges, de bâtiments pour la cavalerie — les carrelages
d'un bleu vif et les chemins de brique rose — les déploie-
ments d'étoffes à loisir, les confitures de roses à miel et le
poulain qui nous est né dans les bagages de l'armée — les

aloud of decrees, and twenty peoples under our law speaking all tongues. . .

"And already you know their favorite tale: the needy captains in immortal paths, the notables crowding to do us obeisance, the whole male population of the year holding aloft its gods on staves, and the princes fallen in the Northern wastes, their daughters tributary swearing fealty to us, and the Master saying: I have faith in my destiny. . .

"Or else you will tell them of the deeds of peace: in countries infested with comfort an odour of forum and of nubile women, the yellow coins of purest ring, fingered under palms, and peoples on the march on strong spices — military endowments, great traffic of influence in the teeth of the rivers, the homage of a powerful neighbour seated in the shadow of his girls, and messages exchanged on leaves of gold, treaties of amity and of boundary, conventions of people with people for damming of streams, and tribute levied in delighted lands! (building of cisterns and of granges and of cavalry barracks — the floors of bright blue and the ways of rose red brick — leisurely unfolding of stuffs, the honey rose jelly and the colt which is born to us among the army gear — the leisurely unfolding of stuffs, and in the mirror of our dreams, the sword-rusting sea, and, one evening, descent into the coast provinces, towards our lands of great ease and towards our

"scented girls, who shall soothe us with a breath, silken webs . . .")

déploiements d'étoffes à loisir et, dans les glaces de nos songes, la mer qui rouille les épées, et la descente, un soir, dans les provinces maritimes, vers nos pays de grand loisir et vers nos filles

"parfumées, qui nous apaiseront d'un souffle, ces tissus . . .")

— Ainsi parfois nos seuils pressés d'un singulier destin et, sur les pas précipités du jour, de ce côté du monde, le plus vaste, où le pouvoir s'exile chaque soir, tout un veuvage de lauriers!

Mais au soir, une odeur de violettes et d'argile, aux mains des filles de nos femmes, nous visitait dans nos projets d'établissement et de fortune

et les vents calmes hébergeaient au fond des golfes désertiques.

— In this wise sometimes our threshold trodden by a strange destiny, and on the hurried steps of day, on this side of the world, the most vast, where power each evening is exiled, all a widowhood of laurels!

But at evening an odour of violets and clay in the hands of our wives' maidens, haunted us in our thoughts of foundation and fortune

and the still winds harboured in the depths of the desert-like gulfs.

VII

Nous n'habiterons pas toujours ces terres jaunes, notre délice...

L'Eté plus vaste que l'Empire suspend aux tables de l'espace plusieurs étages de climats. La terre vaste sur son aire roule à pleins bords sa braise pâle sous les cendres — Couleur de soufre, de miel, couleur de choses immortelles, toute la terre aux herbes s'allumant aux pailles de l'autre hiver — et de l'éponge verte d'un seul arbre le ciel tire son suc violet.

VII

WE SHALL not dwell forever in these yellow lands, our pleasance. . .

The Summer vaster than the Empire hangs over the tables of space several terraces of climate. The huge earth rolls on its surface over-flowing its pale embers under the ashes — Sulphur colour, honey colour, colour of immortal things, the whole grassy earth taking light from the straw of last winter — and from the green sponge of a lonely tree the sky draws its violet juices.

Un lieu de pierres à mica! Pas une graine pure dans les barbes du vent. Et la lumière comme une huile. — De la fissure des paupières au fil des cimes m'unissant, je sais la pierre tachée d'ouies, les essaims du silence aux ruches de lumière; et mon cœur prend souci d'une famille d'acridiens. . .

Chamelles douces sous la tonte, cousues de mauves cicatrices, que les collines s'acheminent sous les données du ciel agraire — qu'elles cheminent en silence sur les incandescences pâles de la plaine; et s'agenouillent à la fin, dans la fumée des songes, là où les peuples s'abolissent aux poudres mortes de la terre.

Ce sont de grandes lignes calmes qui s'en vont à des bleuissements de vignes improbables. La terre en plus d'un point mûrit les violettes de l'orage; et ces fumées de sable qui s'élèvent au lieu des fleuves morts, comme des pans de siècles en voyage. . .

A voix plus basse pour les morts, à voix plus basse dans le jour. Tant de douceur au cœur de l'homme, se peut-il qu'elle faille à trouver sa mesure? . . "Je vous parle, mon âme! — mon âme tout enténébrée d'un parfum de cheval!" Et quelques grands oiseaux de terre, naviguant en Ouest, sont de bons mimes de nos oiseaux de mer.

A l'orient du ciel si pâle, comme un lieu saint scellé des linges de l'aveugle, des nuées calmes se disposent, où

A place of stone of quartz! Not a pure grain in the wind's barbs. And light like oil. — From the crack of my eye to the level of the hills I join myself, I know the stones gillstained, the swarms of silence in the hives of light; and my heart gives heed to a family of crickets. . .

Milch-camels, gentle beneath the shears, sewn with mauve scars, let the hills march forth under the facts of the harvest sky — let them march in silence over the pale incandescence of the plain; and kneeling at last, in the fantasy of dreams, there where the peoples annihilate themselves in the dead powder of earth.

These are the great quiet lines that disperse in the fading blue of doubtful vines. The earth here and there ripens the violets of storm; and these sandsmokes that rise over dead river courses, like the skirts of centuries on their route. . .

Lower voice for the dead, lower voice by day. Such mildness in the heart of man, can it fail to find its measure? . . "I speak to you, my soul! — my soul darkened by the horse smell!" and several great land birds, voyaging westwards, make good likeness of our sea birds.

In the east of so pale a sky, like a holy place sealed by the blind man's linen, calm clouds arrange themselves, where the cancers of camphor and horn revolve. . . Smoke which a

tournent les cancers du camphre et de la corne. . .
Fumées qu'un souffle nous dispute! la terre tout attente en
ses barbes d'insectes, la terre enfante des merveilles! . .

Et à midi, quand l'arbre jujubier fait éclater l'assise
des tombeaux, l'homme clôt ses paupières et rafraîchit sa
nuque dans les âges. . . Cavaleries du songe au lieu des
poudres mortes, ô routes vaines qu'échevèle un souffle
jusqu'à nous! où trouver, où trouver les guerriers qui garde-
ront les fleuves dans leurs noces?

Au bruit des grandes eaux en marche sur la terre,
tout le sel de la terre tressaille dans les songes. Et soudain,
ha! soudain que nous veulent ces voix? Levez un peuple de
miroirs sur l'ossuaire des fleuves, qu'ils interjettent appel
dans la suite des siècles! Levez des pierres à ma gloire, levez
des pierres au silence, et à la garde de ces lieux les cavaleries
de bronze vert sur de vastes chaussées! . . .

(L'ombre d'un grand oiseau me passe sur la face.)

breath of wind claims from us! the earth poised tense in its insect barbs, the earth is brought to bed of wonders! . .

And at noon, when the jujuba tree breaks the tombstone, man closes his lids and cools his neck in the ages. . . Horse-tramplings of dreams in the place of dead powders, O vain ways swept away by a breath, to our feet! where find, where find, the warriors who shall watch the streams in their nuptials?

At the sound of great waters on march over the earth, all the salt of the earth shudders in dream. And sudden, ah sudden, what would these voices with us? Levy a wilderness of mirrors on the boneyard of streams, let them appeal in the course of ages! Erect stones to my fame, erect stones to silence; and to guard these places, cavalcades of green bronze on the great causeways! . . .

(The shadow of a great bird falls on my face.)

VIII

*L*OIS *sur la vente des juments. Lois errantes. Et nous-mêmes. (Couleur d'hommes.)*

Nos compagnons ces hautes trombes en voyage, clepsydres en marche sur la terre,

et les averses solennelles, d'une substance merveilleuse, tissées de poudres et d'insectes, qui poursuivaient nos peuples dans les sables comme l'impôt de capitation.

(A la mesure de nos cœurs fut tant d'absence consommée!)

VIII

LAWS concerning the sale of mares. Nomad laws. And ourselves. (Man colour.)

Our companions these high waterspouts on the march, clepsydrae travelling over the earth,

and the solemn rains, of a marvellous substance, woven of powders and insects, pursuing our folk in the sands like a headtax.

(To the scale of our hearts was such vacance completed!)

*Non que l'étape fût stérile: au pas des bêtes sans al-
liances (nos chevaux purs aux yeux d'aînés), beaucoup de
choses entreprises sur les ténèbres de l'esprit — beaucoup
de choses à loisir sur les frontières de l'esprit — grandes his-
toires séleucides au sifflement des frondes et la terre livrée
aux explications. . .*

*Autre chose: ces ombres — les prévarications du
ciel contre la terre. . .*

*Cavaliers au travers de telles familles humaines, où
les haines parfois chantaient comme des mésanges, lèverons-
nous le fouet sur les mots hongres du bonheur? — Homme,
pèse ton poids calculé en froment. Un pays-ci n'est point le
mien. Que m'a donné le monde que ce mouvement
d'herbes? . .*

*
* *

*Jusqu'au lieu dit de l'Arbre Sec:
    et l'éclair famélique m'assigne ces provinces en Ou-
est.*

*Mais au delà sont les plus grands loisirs, et dans un
grand
    pays d'herbages sans mémoire, l'année sans liens et
sans anniversaires, assaisonnée d'aurores et de feux. (Sacri-
fice au matin d'un cœur de mouton noir.)*

*

*   *

Not that this stage was in vain: to the pace of the eremite beasts (our pure bred horses with eyes of elders) many things undertaken on the darkness of the spirit — infinity of things at leisure on the marches of the spirit — great seleucid histories to the whistling of slings and the earth given over to explanations. . .

And again: these shadows — the prevarications of the sky against the earth. . .

Cavaliers, across such human families, in whom hatreds sang now and then like tomtits, shall we raise our whip over the gelded words of happiness? — Man, weigh your weight measured in wheat. A country here, not mine. What has the world given me but this swaying of grass? . .

*

*   *

To the place called the Place of the Dry Tree:

and the starved levin allots me these provinces in the West.

But beyond are the greater leisures, and in a great

land of grass without memory, the unconfined unreckoned year, seasoned with dawns and heavenly fires. (Matutinal sacrifice of the heart of a black sheep.)

*

*   *

     Chemins du monde, l'un vous suit. Autorité sur tous les signes de la terre.

     O Voyageur dans le vent jaune, goût de l'âme! . . . et la graine, dis-tu, du cocculus indien possède, qu'on la broie! des vertus enivrantes.

*

*   *

     Un grand principe de violence commandait à nos mœurs.

       *

    *   *

Roads of the world, we follow you. Authority over all the signs of the earth.

O Traveller in the yellow wind, lust of the soul! . . and the seed (so you say) of the Indian cocculus possesses (if you mash it!) intoxicating properties.

       *

    *   *

A great principle of violence dictated our fashions.

I X

DEPUIS un si long temps que nous allions en Ouest, que savions-nous des choses

périssables?. . . et soudain à nos pieds les premières fumées. . .

— Jeunes femmes! et la nature d'un pays s'en trouve toute parfumée:

*

* *

"... Je t'annonce les temps d'une grande chaleur et les veuves criardes sur la dissipation des morts.

I X

SUCH a long time now we were making westward, what did we know of those things which are
  perishable? . . and sudden at our feet the first smokes. . .

  — Young women! and the nature of a land is all scented therewith:
*
* *
  ". . . I foretell you the time of great heat, and the widows keening over the dissipation of the dead.

*Ceux qui vieillissent dans l'usage et le soin du si-
lence, assis sur les hauteurs, considèrent les sables*

et la célébrité du jour sur les rades foraines;

*mais le plaisir au flanc des femmes se compose, et
dans nos corps de femmes il y a comme un ferment de raisin
noir, et de répit avec nous-mêmes il n'en est point.*

*". . . Je t'annonce les temps d'une grande faveur
et la félicité des feuilles dans nos songes.*

*Ceux qui savent les sources sont avec nous dans cet
exil; ceux qui savent les sources nous diront-ils au soir*

sous quelles mains pressant la vigne de nos flancs

*nos corps s'emplissent d'une salive? (Et la femme
s'est couchée avec l'homme dans l'herbe; elle se lève, met
ordre aux lignes de son corps, et le criquet s'envole sur son
aile bleue.)*

*". . . Je t'annonce les temps d'une grande chaleur,
et pareillement la nuit, sous l'aboiement des chiens, trait son
plaisir au flanc des femmes.*

*Mais l'Étranger vit sous sa tente, honoré de laitages,
de fruits. On lui apporte de l'eau fraîche*

pour y laver sa bouche, son visage et son sexe.

*On lui mène à la nuit de grandes femmes bréhaignes
(ha! plus nocturnes dans le jour!) Et peut-être aussi de moi
tirera-t-il son plaisir. (Je ne sais quelles sont ses façons
d'être avec les femmes.)*

They who grow old in the custom and the care of silence,
squatting on the heights, contemplate the sands,

and the notoriety of the day over open roadsteads;

but the pleasure forms itself within the womb, and in our
women's bodies there is as a ferment of black grape, and of respite
with ourselves there is not.

". . . I foretell you the time of a great blessing and the
felicity of leaves in our dreams.

Those who know the springs are with us in this exile;
those who know the springs will they tell us at evening

beneath what hands pressing the vine of our wombs

our bodies are filled with a spittle? (And the woman has
lain down with the man in the grass; she rises, arranges the
lines of her body, and the cricket makes off on blue wing.)

". . . I foretell you the time of great heat, and likewise
the night, when the dogs bark, takes its pleasure from the womb
of women.

But the Stranger dwells in his tent, honoured with gifts
of dairy produce and fruit. He is offered fresh water

to wash therewith his mouth, his face and his sex.

At night he is brought tall barren women (more noc-
turnal in the day!) And perhaps of me also will he have his
pleasure. (I know not what are his ways with women.)

". . . Je t'annonce les temps d'une grande faveur et la félicité des sources dans nos songes.

Ouvre ma bouche dans la lumière, ainsi qu'un lieu de miel entre les roches, et si l'on trouve faute en moi, que je sois congédiée! sinon,

que j'aille sous la tente, que j'aille nue, près de la cruche, sous la tente,

et compagnon de l'angle du tombeau, tu me verras longtemps muette sous l'arbre-fille de mes veines. . . Un lit d'instances sous la tente, l'étoile verte dans la cruche, et que je sois sous ta puissance! nulle servante sous la tente que la cruche d'eau fraîche! (Je sais sortir avant le jour sans éveiller l'étoile verte, le criquet sur le seuil et l'aboiement des chiens de toute la terre.)

Je t'annonce les temps d'une grande faveur et la félicité du soir sur nos paupières périssables. . .

mais pour l'instant encore c'est le jour!"

*

* *

— et debout sur la tranche éclatante du jour, au seuil d'un grand pays plus chaste que la mort,

les filles urinaient en écartant la toile peinte de leur robe.

". . . I foretell you the time of great blessing, and the felicity of fountains in our dreams.

Open my mouth in the light, as a honey store among the rocks, and if fault be found in me, let me be dismissed! otherwise

may I enter in under the tent, may I enter naked, near the cruse, under the tent,

and companion of the grave-corner, you shall see me for long time unspeaking under virgin branches of my veins. . . A bed of entreaties under the tent, the green star in the cruse, and may I be under your dominion! no serving-maid under the tent but the cruse of cool water! (I have ways to depart before day without wakening the green star, the cricket on the threshold and the baying of the dogs of the whole world.)

I foretell you the time of great blessing and the bounty of the evening on our eyelids that endure not. . .

but for the time being it is still day!"

*
* *

— and erect on the shining edge of the day, on the threshold of a great land more chaste than death,

the girls made water straddling and holding aside their print gowns.

X

*F*AIS choix d'un grand chapeau dont on séduit le
bord. L'œil recule d'un siècle aux provinces de l'âme. Par la
porte de craie vive on voit les choses de la plaine: choses
vivantes, ô choses
     excellentes!

     des sacrifices de poulains sur des tombes d'enfants,
des purifications de veuves dans les roses et des rassemble-
ments d'oiseaux verts dans les cours en l'honneur des vieil-
lards;

X

SELECT a wide hat with the brim seduced. The eye withdraws by a century into the provinces of the soul. Through the gate of living chalk we see the things of the plain: living things,

excellent things!

sacrifice of colts on the tombs of children, purification of widows among the roses and consignments of green birds in the courtyards to do honour to the old men;

beaucoup de choses sur la terre à entendre et à voir,
choses vivantes parmi nous!

des célébrations de fêtes en plein air pour des anni-
versaires de grands arbres et des cérémonies publiques en
l'honneur d'une mare; des dédicaces de pierres noires, par-
faitement rondes, des inventions de sources en lieux morts,
des consécrations d'étoffes, à bout de perches, aux approches
des cols, et des acclamations violentes, sous les murs, pour
des mutilations d'adultes au soleil, pour des publications de
linges d'épousailles!

bien d'autres choses encore à hauteur de nos tempes:
les pansements de bêtes au faubourgs, les mouvements de
foules au devant des tondeurs, des puisatiers et des hon-
greurs; les spéculations au souffle des moissons et la ven-
tilation d'herbages, à bout de fourches, sur les toits; les con-
structions d'enceintes de terre cuite et rose, de sècheries de
viandes en terrasses, de galeries pour les prêtres, de capi-
taineries; les cours immenses du vétérinaire; les corvées
d'entretien de routes muletières, de chemins en lacets dans
les gorges; les fondations d'hospices en lieux vagues;
les écritures à l'arrivée des caravanes et les licenciements
d'escortes aux quartiers de changeurs; les popularités nais-
santes sous l'auvent, devant les cuves à fritures; les protesta-
tions de titres de créance; les destructions de bêtes albinos,
de vers blancs sous la terre, les feux de ronces et d'épines
aux lieux souillés de mort, la fabrication d'un beau pain

many things on the earth to hear and to see, living things among us!

celebrations of open air festivals for the name-day of great trees and public rites in honour of a pool; consecration of black stones perfectly round, water-dowsing in dead places, dedication of cloths held up on poles, at the gates of the passes, and loud acclamations under the walls for the mutilation of adults in the sun, for the publication of the bride-sheets!

many other things too at the level of our eyes: dressing the sores of animals in the suburbs, stirring of the crowds before sheep-shearers, well-sinkers and horse-gelders; speculations in the breath of harvests and turning of hay on the roofs, on the prongs of forks; building of enclosures of rose red terra cotta, of terraces for meat-drying, of galleries for priests, of quarters for captains; the vast court of the horse-doctor; the fatigue parties for upkeep of muleways, of zig-zag roads through the gorges; foundation of hospices in vacant places; the invoicing at arrival of caravans, and disbanding of escorts in the quarter of money-changers; budding popularities under the penthouse, in front of the frying vats; protestation of bills of credit; destruction of albino animals, of white worms in the soil; fires of bramble and thorn in places defiled by death, the making of a fine bread of barley and sesame; or else of spelt; and the firesmoke of mankind everywhere. . .

d'orge et de sésame; ou bien d'épeautre; et la fumée des hommes en tous lieux. . .

     ha! toutes sortes d'hommes dans leurs voies et façons: mangeurs d'insectes, de fruits d'eau; porteurs d'emplâtres, de richesses; l'agriculteur et l'adalingue, l'acuponcteur et le saunier; le péager, le forgeron; marchands de sucre, de cannelle, de coupes à boire en métal blanc et de lampes de corne; celui qui taille un vêtement de cuir, des sandales dans le bois et des boutons en forme d'olives; celui qui donne à la terre ses façons; et l'homme de nul métier: homme au faucon, homme à la flûte, homme aux abeilles; celui qui tire son plaisir du timbre de sa voix, celui qui trouve son emploi dans la contemplation d'une pierre verte; qui fait brûler pour son plaisir un feu d'écorces sur son toit; qui se fait sur la terre un lit de feuilles odorantes, qui s'y couche et repose; qui pense à des dessins de céramiques vertes pour des bassins d'eaux vives; et celui qui a fait des voyages et songe à repartir; qui a vécu dans un pays de grandes pluies; qui joue aux dés, aux osselets, au jeu des gobelets; ou qui a déployé sur le sol ses tables à calcul; celui qui a des vues sur l'emploi d'une calebasse; celui qui traîne un aigle mort comme un faix de branchages sur ses pas (et la plume est donnée, non vendue, pour l'empennage des flèches), celui qui récolte le pollen dans un vaisseau de bois (et mon plaisir, dit-il, est dans cette couleur jaune); celui qui mange des beignets, des vers de palmes, des framboises;

ha! all conditions of men in their ways and manners; eaters of insects, of water fruits; those who bear poultices, those who bear riches; the husbandman, and the young noble horsed; the healer with needles, and the salter; the toll-gatherer, the smith; vendors of sugar, of cinnamon, of white metal drinking cups and of lanthorns; he who fashions a leather tunic, wooden shoes and olive-shaped buttons; he who dresses a field; and the man of no trade: the man with the falcon, the man with the flute, the man with bees; he who has his delight in the pitch of his voice, he who makes it his business to contemplate a green stone; he who burns for his pleasure a thornfire on his roof; he who makes on the ground his bed of sweet-smelling leaves, lies down there and rests; he who thinks out designs of green pottery for fountains; and he who has travelled far and dreams of departing again; he who has dwelt in a country of great rains; the dicer, the knuckle-bone player, the juggler; or he who has spread on the ground his reckoning tablets; he who has his opinions on the use of a gourd; he who drags a dead eagle like a faggot on his tracks (and the plumage is given, not sold, for fletching); he who gathers pollen in a wooden jar (and my delight, says he, is in this yellow colour); he who eats fritters, the maggots of the palmtree, or raspberries; he who fancies the flavour of tarragon; he who dreams of green pepper, or else he who chews fossil gum, who lifts a conch to his ear, or he who sniffs the odour of genius in the freshly cracked

celui qui aime le goût de l'estragon; celui qui rêve d'un poivron; ou bien encore celui qui mâche d'une gomme fossile, qui porte une conque à son oreille, et celui qui épie le parfum de génie aux cassures fraîches de la pierre; celui qui pense au corps de femme, homme libidineux; celui qui voit son âme au reflet d'une lame; l'homme versé dans les sciences, dans l'onomastique; l'homme en faveur dans les conseils, celui qui nomme les fontaines, qui fait un don de sièges sous les arbres, de laines teintes pour les sages; et fait sceller aux carrefours de très grands bols de bronze pour la soif; bien mieux, celui qui ne fait rien, tel homme et tel dans ses façons, et tant d'autres encore! les ramasseurs de cailles dans les plis de terrains, ceux qui récoltent dans les broussailles les œufs tiquetés de vert, ceux qui descendent de cheval pour ramasser des choses, des agates, une pierre bleu pâle que l'on taille à l'entrée des faubourgs (en manière d'étuis, de tabatières et d'agrafes, ou de boules à rouler aux mains des paralytiques); ceux qui peignent en sifflant des coffrets en plein air, l'homme au bâton d'ivoire, l'homme à la chaise de rotin, l'ermite orné de mains de fille et le guerrier licencié qui a planté sa lance sur son seuil pour attacher un singe . . . ha! toutes sortes d'hommes dans leurs voies et façons, et soudain! apparu dans ses vêtements du soir et tranchant à la ronde toutes questions de préséance, le Conteur qui prend place au pied du térébinthe . . .

O généalogiste sur la place! combien d'histoires de

stone; he who thinks of the flesh of women, the lustful; he who sees his soul reflected in a blade; the man learned in sciences, in onomastic; the man well thought of in councils, he who names fountains, he who makes a public gift of seats in the shady places, of dyed wool for the wise men; and has great bronze jars, for thirst, planted at the crossways; better still, he who does nothing, such a one and such in his manners, and so many others still! those who collect quails in the wrinkled land, those who hunt among the furze for green-speckled eggs, those who dismount to pick things up, agates, a pale blue stone which they cut and fashion at the gates of the suburbs (into cases, tobacco-boxes, brooches, or into balls to be rolled between the hands of the paralysed); those who whistling paint boxes in the open air, the man with the ivory staff, the man with the rattan chair, the hermit with hands like a girl's and the disbanded warrior who has planted his spear at the threshold to tie up a monkey . . . ha! all sorts of men in their ways and fashions, and of a sudden! behold in his evening robes and summarily settling in turn all questions of precedence, the Story-Teller who stations himself at the foot of the turpentine tree . . .

O genealogist upon the market-place! how many chronicles of families and connexions? — and may the dead seize the quick, as is said in the tables of the law, if I have not seen each thing in its own shadow and the virtue of its age: the stores of books and annals, the astronomer's storehouses and the beauty of

familles et de filiations? — et que le mort saisisse le vif,
comme il est dit aux tables du légiste, si je n'ai vu toute chose
dans son ombre et le mérite de son âge: les entrepôts de livres
et d'annales, les magasins de l'astronome et la beauté d'un
lieu de sépultures, de très vieux temples sous les palmes,
habités d'une mule et de trois poules blanches — et par delà
le cirque de mon œil, beaucoup d'actions secrètes en chemin:
les campements levés sur des nouvelles qui m'échappent, les
effronteries de peuples aux collines et les passages de rivières
sur des outres; les cavaliers porteurs de lettres d'alliance,
l'embuscade dans les vignes, les entreprises de pillards au
fond des gorges et les manœuvres à travers champs pour le
rapt d'une femme, les marchandages et les complots, l'ac-
couplement de bêtes en forêt sous les yeux des enfants, et
des convalescences de prophètes au fond des bouveries, les
conversations muettes de deux hommes sous un arbre . . .

    mais par dessus les actions des hommes sur la terre,
beaucoup de signes en voyage, beaucoup de graines en
voyage, et sous l'azyme du beau temps, dans un grand
souffle de la terre, toute la plume des moissons! . .

    jusqu'à l'heure du soir où l'étoile femelle, chose pure
et gagée dans les hauteurs du ciel . . .

    Terre arable du songe! Qui parle de bâtir? — J'ai
vu la terre distribuée en de vastes espaces et ma pensée n'est
point distraite du navigateur.

a place of sepulture, of very old temples under the palmtrees, frequented by a mule and three white hens — and beyond my eye's circuit, many a secret doing on the routes: striking of camps upon tidings which I know not, effronteries of the hill tribes, and passage of rivers on skin-jars; horsemen bearing letters of alliance, the ambush in the vineyard, forays of robbers in the depths of gorges and manoeuvres over field to ravish a woman, bargain-driving and plots, coupling of beasts in the forests before the eyes of children, convalescence of prophets in byres, the silent talk of two men under a tree . . .

but over and above the actions of men on the earth, many omens on the way, many seeds on the way, and under unleavened fine weather, in one great breath of the earth, the whole feather of harvest! . .

until the hour of evening when the female star, pure and pledged in the sky heights . . .

Plough-land of dream! Who talks of building? — I have seen the earth parcelled out in vast spaces and my thought is not heedless of the navigator.

CHANSON

SONG

MON CHEVAL arrêté sous l'arbre plein de tour-
terelles, je siffle un sifflement si pur, qu'il n'est promesses à
leurs rives que tiennent tous ces fleuves (Feuilles vivantes au
matin sont à l'image de la gloire). . .

*

Et ce n'est point qu'un homme ne soit triste, mais se
levant avant le jour et se tenant avec prudence dans le com-
merce d'un vieil arbre, appuyé du menton à la dernière
étoile, il voit au fond du ciel à jeun de grandes choses pures
qui tournent au plaisir. . .

*

Mon cheval arrêté sous l'arbre qui roucoule, je siffle
un sifflement plus pur. . . Et paix à ceux, s'ils vont mourir,

I HAVE halted my horse by the tree of the doves, I whistle a note so sweet, shall the rivers break faith with their banks? (Living leaves in the morning fashioned in glory)...

*

And not that a man be not sad, but arising before day and biding circumspectly in the communion of an old tree, leaning his chin on the last fading star, he beholds at the end of the fasting sky great things and pure that unfold to delight . . .

*

I have halted my horse by the dove-moaning tree, I whistle a note more sweet . . . Peace to the dying who have not

*qui n'ont point vu ce jour. Mais de mon frère le poète on a
eu des nouvelles. Il a écrit encore une chose très douce. Et
quelques-uns en eurent connaissance. . .*

seen this day! But tidings there are of my brother the poet: once more he has written a song of great sweetness. And some there are who have knowledge thereof . . .

BIBLIOGRAPHY

I

THE WORKS OF ST.-JOHN PERSE

IN FRENCH AND FOREIGN EDITIONS

ÉLOGES

French Editions
> First edition: Paris, N.R.F., Marcel Rivière, 1911
> Second edition: Paris, N.R.F., Gallimard, 1925
> Third edition: Paris, N.R.F., Gallimard, 1948 (Edition revised and corrected by the author)

American Edition
> ELOGES AND OTHER POEMS, French text with English translation by Louise Varèse, introduction by Archibald MacLeish, New York, W. W. Norton and Co., 1944

Spanish Editions
> 1. Paris, 1913 (ELOGIOS, version castellana de Ricardo Guiraldes)
> 2. Mexico, Costa-Amic, 1946 (ELOGIOS Y OTROS POEMAS, version castellana de Jorge Zalamea)

AMITIÉ DU PRINCE

French Edition
> Paris, Ronald Davis, 1924

ANABASE

French Editions
> 1. In France
> First edition: Paris, N.R.F., Gallimard, 1924

Second edition: Paris, N.R.F., Gallimard, 1925
Third edition: Paris, Gallimard, 1947
Fourth edition: Paris, Gallimard, 1948 (Edition revised and corrected by the author)
2. In the U.S.A.
New York, Brentano's, 1945

English Edition

London, Faber & Faber, Ltd., 1930 (ANABASIS, French text with English translation and preface by T. S. Eliot)

American Editions

First edition: New York, Harcourt, Brace and Co., 1938 (ANABASIS, French text with English translation and preface by T. S. Eliot. The translation revised and corrected by T. S. Eliot for this American edition)

Second edition: New York, Harcourt, Brace and Co., 1949 (ANABASIS, French text with English translation, preface and additional note by T. S. Eliot. The translation again revised and corrected by T. S. Eliot for this new American edition)

German Editions

1. Leipzig, Insel-Verlag, 1929 (ANABASIS, German translation by Bernard Groethuysen and Walter Benjamin, with preface by Hugo von Hofmannsthal) (Publication suspended)
2. Bühl-Baden, Roland-Verlag, 1948 (ANABASIS, French text with German translation and introductory note by Kurt Wais)

Russian Edition

Paris, J. Povolovsky, 1926 (ANABASIS, Russian translation by G. Adamowitch and G. Ivanoff, with preface by Valéry Larbaud)

Italian Edition

Rome, Edizione di *Novissima*, 1936 (ANABASIS, Italian translation, with preface, by Giuseppe Ungaretti)

Spanish Editions

1. Mexico—First edition: Contemporeneos, 1931 (ANABASIS, French text with Spanish translation, and preface, by Octavio J. Barreda)

—Second edition: Letras de Mexico, 1940 (ANABASIS, French text with Spanish translation, and preface, by Octavio J. Barreda)
2. Bogota, 1949 (ANABASIS, version castellana de Jorge Zalamea)

Roumanian Edition
Bucarest, Cartea Romanesca, 1932 (ANABASIS, Roumanian translation, with preface, by Ion Pillat)

EXIL, SUIVI DE POÈME A L'ÉTRANGÈRE, PLUIES, NEIGES

French Editions
1. In Argentina
Buenos Aires, Lettres Françaises, 1944 (QUATRE POEMES, 1941-1944)
2. In Switzerland
Neuchâtel, Editions de La Baconnière, 1943 (EXIL)
3. In France
First Edition: Paris, N.R.F., Gallimard, 1945 (EXIL, POÈME A L'ÉTRANGÈRE, PLUIES, NEIGES)
Second Edition: Paris, N.R.F., Gallimard, 1946 (Edition revised and corrected by the author)

Spanish Edition
Milan (Italy), Italgeo, 1946 (LLUVIAS, NIEVES, EXILIO, version castellana de Jorge Zalamea. Illustraciones de Luna)

Italian Edition
Milan, 1949 (to be published, at Mondadori) (Italian translations by Giuseppe Ungaretti and Renato Poggioli)

German Edition
Berlin, Karl Henssel Verlag, 1949 (EXIL, GEDICHT AN EINE FREMDE, REGEN, SCHNEE, German translations by L. Ringelnatz and Wolfgang Rüttenauer)

American Edition
EXILE AND OTHER POEMS, bilingual edition, translation by Denis Devlin, New York, The Bollingen Series, Pantheon Books, 1949

VENTS

French Edition
Paris, N.R.F., Gallimard, 1946

II

ANABASIS

First publication in the French review *La Nouvelle Revue Française*, Paris, 1924.

First edition: Paris, N.R.F., Gallimard, 1924.

The second edition (Paris, N.R.F., Gallimard, 1925) was published in a de luxe edition, *grand in-folio*, of very large format. printed with special type by Maurice Darantière, Dijon, France.

Between 1925 and 1947, date of the third edition (Paris, N.R.F., Gallimard), no French re-issue has ever been authorized by the author.

The fourth French edition (Paris, N.R.F., Gallimard, 1948) was revised and corrected by the author.

On the following pages are three Prefaces published with foreign editions of *Anabasis*.

PREFACE BY VALERY LARBAUD[1]

AT FIRST SIGHT nothing would seem more personal than poetic works. They isolate themselves and they oppose, contradict and exclude one another. Yet within the limits of each language the great monuments of the poetic art form an architectural whole, which is the richer and the more surprising because each individual monument differs from the others. This whole endures, nor can any fragment of it be detached. We speak of English poetry, of French poetry and of Spanish poetry, even at periods when these different poetries were closely inter-related. This is no result of the so-called national genius, but of the linguistic laws which govern the development of each literary language.

Théophile de Viau, writing of Malherbe, declared:

Malherbe a très bien fait, mais il a fait pour lui
Malherbe wrought well, but for his sake alone

and, as he was writing, Viau believed that he too "wrought for his sake alone," whereas he was adding his lyric monument to Malherbe's amid a group that includes Lingendes, Etienne Durand and Racan.

Within each linguistic field we must make an inventory, every thirty years or so, of the poetic monuments which have remained standing whilst others, set up at the same period, have crumbled to ruins.

How many French poets were read between 1895 and 1925? Possibly a hundred, of whom thirty at least seem worthy of attention and qualified to add something to the ensemble of French poetry.

[1] Preface written for the 1926 Russian edition of *Anabasis*. Published in the *Nouvelle Revue Française,* Volume CXLVII, January 1926, under the title of "Preface for an Edition of *Anabase.*"

The period was one of feverish activity. Poets were completing the dislocation of the Alexandrine, freeing this measure from classical tyranny of versification. Free verse was in the process of invention. The laws of the *"verset"* were being explored. Experiments were being conducted with a view to combining the rhythms of prose with the rhythms of lyric poetry. A host of craftsmen were copying the monuments of the past, trying to rejuvenate them.

What remains of all this effort? How many lasting monuments did all this labor add to the sum of French poetry? They may be counted on the fingers of one hand.

We have the enormous lyrical and dramatic monument of Paul Claudel which dominates the entire group; that of Paul Valéry; that of Francis Jammes, so traditional in character that we must enter within to appreciate its novelty and the personal contribution it brought to the treasure-store of French lyricism; that of Léon-Paul Fargue, with its lofty tower and graceful portal, wherein we recover the baroque ornamentation of Baudelaire's balcony and the enlivening influence of Rimbaud's inner romanticism; and finally, the more recently added, and still unfinished, monument of St.-John Perse: his *Eloges* and his *Anabase*. . . .

In thirty years, then, we have five monuments, as against some fivescore buildings which stand in ruins about them or which have crumbled to dust. What a terrible and silent Judgment!

Yet all these attempts were not in vain. Noble fragments of some of them persist which, in the years to come, will interest such rarely privileged archeologists as can appreciate their beauty, regardless of the historic value of documents. The fact remains, however, that only the works of Claudel, Valéry, Jammes, Fargue and St.-John Perse endure today and will continue to endure.

(When all is said and done, did the age of Henry IV, one of the most productive of literary eras, bequeath us a greater number?)

A personal poetic thought is perforce a novel thought, indeed a foreign thought. Faced with Claudel's earliest works, many belated literati — I mean men not sufficiently well-lettered — felt that they were reading translations and imitations of foreign works. Today it is obvious that nothing could possibly be more French than the matter and form of

Claudel's writings. The same will hold true of St.-John Perse's poetic vision and of his prosody, based on the Alexandrine.

Indeed, what he has brought to French lyricism, what he has described and what he has introduced into French poetry is very novel and very personal. He has offered geographic, historic and human visions of the lands in which he has lived (the West Indies, where he spent his childhood, and China, where he resided several years). In *Anabase*, he gives the chronicle of an ascent from the shores of the sea to the deserts of Central Asia:

> *Milch-camels, gentle beneath the shears, sewn with mauve scars, let the hills march forth under the facts of the harvest sky — let them march in silence over the pale incandescence of the plain; and kneeling at last, in the fantasy of dreams, there where the peoples annihilate themselves in the dead powder of earth.*

Again, having glimpsed them across our dreams, we cannot fail to recognize:

> *Cavalcades of green bronze on the great causeways . . .*

But what a vast progress, what a renewal, and what a gain in lyric depth since the day of Chateaubriand's descriptions! Those of St.-John Perse are at once more exact and precise, they are more highly charged with sense and meditation. These landscapes of his lie within himself; he beholds them in a mirror which rests in the core of his consciousness; he sees them and is astonished; he takes possession of them yet he feels himself alien; an alien on the human plane, not nationally speaking. He is a man to whom our planet will forever be a thing of wonder. It is as if some part of him could not accept the conditions in which he is forced to live as conditions which are his, and made for him, and the only possible ones. Even that "colour of man" which he loves, he perceives and feels as an alien thing.

The language and rhythm, which he compels to express his thought, he treats with the same detachment, a detachment more immaterial and intellectual than haughty. In his hands the language of French poetry is like some splendid thoroughbred he is riding; he uses its qualities but forces it to move at a gait new to it and contrary to its habits.

It is as though he said to the language:

"You shall describe what you never described before I came . . . you shall patiently enumerate objects and actions and men that neither Scève nor Ronsard had observed and that Malherbe and La Fontaine would have considered outside your province . . . you shall set your scale to the scale of this huge Continent, of this far-flung expanse which has nothing to do with the land where you were born and where you grew up. . . ."

Already in *Eloges* St.-John Perse had made this language describe the seas and islands of the tropics. Now, with *Anabase*, he achieves the conquest of Asia, the vast roof of the world. Yet it is the tongue of Scève and Ronsard and La Fontaine and Racine, and it is the line created by Malherbe, which he employs and marshals for his conquest.

Accordingly, if we pause to survey the various architectural units set up in the other great linguistic fields, where shall we find any to match this planetary monument of poesy?

VALÉRY LARBAUD
(*Translated by Jacques Le Clercq, 1949*)

PREFACE BY HUGO VON HOFMANNSTHAL[1]

FOR CLOSE ON forty years we have been watching French poets engaged in a struggle. This struggle and its aim we must attempt to understand — for who, if not we, should be able to do so? Yet it would be of no avail to speak here of schools, tendencies, esthetic fashions or in other such terms whereby literary criticism is wont to obscure the facts.

What is at stake is the French language in its most secret function, and this struggle is an old one. The spirit of this nation, so successfully composed of three ethnical elements, is vivacious but sober. Reason reigns. Towards the end of the seventeenth century this predominance of reason is raised to the fundamental law of the nation. With Malherbe's triumph over Regnier, the reign of reason is forever assured, the flood of the unconscious repressed. Any ambiguous use of language is repudiated and lucidity of the written word is established as the order of the day. Even allegorical expression, the metaphor, is subjected to the severest restrictions. The execution of this law is placed under a final judgment: that of good taste, a kind of intellectual conscience.

The most secret life of language, however — on which the delicate, innermost vitality of a nation depends — offers resistance.

That ancient struggle conducted during the sixteenth century by the Pléiade — the struggle for a free syntax, for richer and more daring metaphors, for closer ties with the music of the epoch, we find resumed towards the end of the nineteenth century. Of this movement Mallarmé is the great leader and theoretician. (But his doctrine resembles his poetry: working through allusion, avoiding precision and logical contexts, its

---

[1] Published in German in the *Neue Schweizer Rundschau*, May, 1929, under the title, "Introduction to St.-J. Perse's *Anabasis*." Published in French in *Commerce*, xx, Eté 1929, under the title, "Emancipation du Lyrisme français."

impact is all the greater and more lasting.) Mallarmé is preceded by the majestic flow, the mysterious polyphony of Baudelaire, by Rimbaud's savage revolt against all order. A common attraction towards music makes both these poets brothers of Mallarmé. For he was, in fact, hardly less musician than poet; from the viewpoint of composition it is almost impossible to detect a difference between Mallarmé and Debussy. Here, too, belong the rhythms of Paul Claudel — one verse, one line of repartee from whose hymns and dramas suffice to bring before us the magic of other worlds. Only to the superficial eye does Valéry's poetry seem to abide by different laws; and this simply because his clarity is so great, because the curve of his language can be expressed almost in mathematical terms. Yet has not Light the same secrets, the same rich recesses as the shadows of evening?

All these poets — and what a line of illustrious names have we not mentioned! — are concerned with the renewal of lyrical inspiration from the heart of language itself. The creative individual, enclosed as in a prison by outworn means of expression, throws himself into language in an effort to find in it the ecstasy of inspiration and new avenues into life — a condition similar to that produced by the hallucinations which swamp the senses after they have been freed from the conscious mind.

This is and always has been the Latin approach towards the unconscious: not one of half-dreamy reveling as that of the Germanic spirit, whereof English as well as German poetry offers such striking examples, but one of violent abandon, a frenzy — a shaking up of values, a shattering of the established order.

These are the saturnalia of the mind. New reflexes appear, visions of a violence barely tolerable to the eye; it is a rejuvenation without parallel, a veritable mystery. Here runs a road which leads from Rimbaud's *Bateau Ivre* to the earliest verses of Stefan George. Both share what the Romans described with the word *incantatio* — the dark and violent self-enchantment induced by the magic of sound and rhythm.

To the most profound tendencies of these poets should be added the work of a contemporary lyricist: St.-John Perse — whose poetic masterpiece we offer here. His *Anabasis* has a heroic background which in its lighter aspects is reminiscent of the severe delicacy of Poussin. The action itself dispenses with historical, ideological or social allusions. The precision that we consider as almost synonymous with the French spirit is eliminated. Less, however, than with Mallarmé do we find the parallel of musical expression: instead of the mirroring-word material so rich in sensual significance, thanks to which the appearance of objects seems to be wrapped in music, we experience great reserve and hardness. Evocative of purity and severity, of domination and self-control, the following words occur again and again: scalebeam; pure salt; the pure idea; the cleansing and sanctifying qualities of salt — *les délices du sel*. The deliberate harshness of transitions, the brusque and repeated disruption of images, the capricious evocation of the Orient — the combination of these qualities constitute a work which alternately offers of itself as much as it withdraws. On closer investigation we find it a poem full of beauty and strength; a work created, moreover — although we cannot say precisely why — in the spirit of our day, that alert and heroic spirit of contemporary France which is giving birth to new saints and founding a new colonial empire before its southern gates.

I am speaking of the original of St.-John Perse's work, not of the translation: a work of this kind is frankly untranslatable. Baudelaire, despite constantly repeated efforts, has never been translated. In such cases translations can do no more than offer a very exact and conscientious report. Nevertheless there does remain a certain fascination in the arrangement of content; but for this fact the attraction, the enchantment of Chinese poems in translation — translations into English and German made not even from the original, but from Latin transcriptions — would be incomprehensible.

HUGO VON HOFMANNSTHAL
(*Translated by James Stern, 1949*)

PREFACE BY GIUSEPPE UNGARETTI[1]

THE *Anabasis* of Perse attracted me for reasons I expressed on the occasion of its first publication in Italian, in the second issue of *Fronte*, in 1931:

"This *Anabasis* which I present in Italian garb is one of the rare recent examples of epic poetry.

"It is an audacious, successful effort to blend the representation of the experiences of a people with a lyric motion, that is, with the story of one I, of the Stranger: *by the roads of all the earth the Stranger to his ways*.

"And the genius of the poet has chosen for his fantasy those places which, *from the valleys and the uplands and the highest slopes of this world to the shores' end*, possess one of the conditions of legendary life: space. The region he evokes has one further epic requirement: his people are *of little weight in the memory of these lands*, that is, the vastness of space preserves them almost primitive in custom, almost innocent in intent.

"Because nature dominates civilization, and man is at the mercy of the elements rather than of his own works, there history matters, not people. Because man, being at grips with nature in an elemental way, is bound to himself and to his fellows by almost uniquely instinctive and religious chains, there the obscurity of natural phenomena signifies, there the fury of the sun, the variables of climate, the inhospitable wind, the spectacle of the progressive desiccation of the earth, the straining of a convoy behind a trickle of water . . .

[1] Preface written for the Italian translation, published in 1931 and 1936.

"There thirst matters, thought for dreams has meaning. *The Stranger has laid his finger on the mouth of the Dead.*"

GIUSEPPE UNGARETTI
(*Translated by Adrienne Foulke, 1949*)

Distinguished books of poetry
available in paperbound editions from
Harcourt Brace Jovanovich, Inc.

Maxwell Anderson	Four Verse Plays (HB 25)
Aristophanes	Four Comedies (HB 51)
Wolf Biermann	The Wire Harp: Ballads, Poems, Songs (HB 141)
C. P. Cavafy	The Complete Poems of Cavafy (HB 108)
E. E. Cummings	E. E. Cummings: A Selection of Poems (HB 92)
T. S. Eliot	The Cocktail Party (HB 69)
	The Confidential Clerk (HB 70)
	The Family Reunion (HB 71)
	Four Quartets (HB 136)
	Murder in the Cathedral (HB 72)
	Old Possum's Book of Practical Cats (HPL 31)
	Selected Poems (HPL 21)
	The Waste Land and Other Poems (HB 1)
William Empson	Collected Poems (HB 38)